ANGELS, ANGELS ALL AROUND

BOB HARTMAN

Illustrations by Jessica Curtis

A LION PAPERBACK

Copyright © 1993 Bob Hartman
Illustrations copyright © 1995 Jessica Curtis
This edition copyright © 1995 Lion Publishing

The author asserts the moral right
to be identified as the author of this work

Published by
Lion Publishing plc
Sandy Lane West, Oxford, England
ISBN 0 7459 3212 6
Albatross Books Pty Ltd
PO Box 320, Sutherland, NSW 2232, Australia
ISBN 0 7324 1227 7

Text first published 1993
This edition first published 1995
10 9 8 7 6 5 4 3 2 1 0

Printed and bound in Great Britain
by Cox & Wyman Ltd, Reading

$\mathscr{C}$ONTENTS

$\mathcal{I}$NTRODUCTION

More than 400 years ago, a woman known as Teresa of Avila said that she was visited by angels. She wrote about the angels she had seen. One, she said, was small of stature and most beautiful. Its face was like fire.

And then Teresa made a guess—a guess that was like fire for me, because it sparked the idea that set this book going. Each angel, she guessed, must surely be one of a kind—each different from every other angel!

I think Teresa was right.

Oh, I suppose angels could be just shiny, winged clones, appearing like heavenly robots to do their jobs and then disappearing with a programmed sameness. But that doesn't seem to fit the way God works in the rest of his creation. He builds wonderful variety into everything else he makes. So why not angels, too?

For that reason, the angels you will meet in these pages don't look much like one another. Some are lumbering hulks. Others are delicate sprites. Some are fierce, others gentle. Some are enormous and some, like Teresa's angel, are beautiful and small. And, yes, some even have wings. But only some.

How have I guessed at their differences? In the original Bible accounts, there are hints about what they might have looked like or how they might have done their jobs. I have tried to be as faithful as possible to those hints.

But I have done some imagining, too, on the basis of the jobs the angels were sent to do. Daniel, for example, finds himself rescued by an angel who really knows how to handle lions. And Peter couldn't hope for a craftier companion to spring him from Herod's prison.

At the end of each story, I have noted the place in the Bible where you can find the original account, so you can read each for yourself. Then you can do some guessing and imagining of your own.

Even though they may be quite different from each other in appearance, all angels are alike in some important ways. They are all God's messengers, God's servants. And they are bound by a common assignment: to encourage, help and guide people like Mary and Hagar and Paul and the Bethlehem shepherds—and people like you and me.

And that, finally, is the most important thing that these stories have to say: God not only sent angels *once upon a time*, he is sending them still. The ancient words of a biblical psalm are as true now as when they were written: "The angel of the Lord encamps around those who fear him, and delivers them."

Or, to put it another way, there are angels, angels all around!

Bob Hartman
Ben Avon, Pennyslvania

$\mathcal{T}$HE FOURTH VULTURE

One vulture.

Hagar saw him out of the corner of her eye as she raised the water pouch to her son's cracked lips.

Empty. The water was all gone.

And the vulture celebrated with a shrill cry and a lazy loop-de-loop.

Two vultures.

Their wings beat slow and heavy, like hot wind against a tent flap.

Hagar heard them as she picked up little Ishmael and laid him in the scraggly shadow of a desert bush. The bread was gone, too. And with it, any hope for survival. Hagar cradled her son's head and stroked one sunken cheek.

"Quiet now," she said. "Sleep now."

And in no time, the exhausted boy was off. Hagar gave him a dry kiss, eased his head onto a rolled-up blanket, and sat down a short distance away. She could

not bear to watch him die, but she could shield him from the sun's hot stare. And she could chase away the vultures.

Three vultures.

Hagar cursed them, shaking her fist at the sky. But they took no notice. They just chased each other, tracing circles round the face of the sun.

Hagar cursed the sun, too. And the desert—this dry and empty place she was forced to wander.

And then she cursed the day that had brought her here—that day so long ago when everything had seemed simple...

She had been a servant girl. And Sarah was her mistress. Sarah, the wife of Abraham—leader of the tribe. Abraham, who had left the comforts of city life to find a new land, a land that God had promised to show him.

God had made another promise, too, so they said. Abraham and Sarah would have a son who would be the first child of a mighty new nation. But Abraham and Sarah weren't getting any younger. Indeed Sarah was already well past her child-bearing years.

And that's where Hagar came in.

"Go to my husband," Sarah had ordered her, "and bear his child. I am too old. God's promise is surely not for me. But perhaps through you, Abraham will see the promise come true."

Hagar had obeyed her mistress. She had given birth to Ishmael. And, for a time, everyone had been happy. Then, several years later, Sarah miraculously became pregnant too, and gave birth to a son she called Isaac. From that moment, Hagar's happiness had begun to flicker and fade, till it finally disappeared like a desert mirage.

Sarah's jealousy was the problem. She feared that Ishmael and not Isaac would receive Abraham's inheritance, because he had been born first. So she made life miserable for Hagar and Ishmael, and finally persuaded Abraham to send them away into the desert.

So now, along with the desert and the vultures and the sun, Hagar cursed Sarah, her jealous mistress. She nearly cursed Abraham, too. Abraham, her master and the father of her son. But then she remembered that look in his eyes as he sent her away.

The look that said, "I don't want to do this."

The look that said, "I can't find any other way."

The look that said, "I believe things will be all right."

Were those looks real? Hagar wondered. Or were they just mirages? Were those tears in the old man's eyes? Or just a reflection of the desert sun?

Four vultures.

And the fourth bigger than the rest.

What did it matter, anyway? thought Hagar. In a short time, both she and Ishmael would be dead. The vultures would get their dinner. Sarah would get her way. And Abraham would still get what his God had promised—a son, a family, a mighty nation.

Abraham's God had been good to him. Oh, that he would be so good to her.

And yet there had been a time, Hagar remembered, a time when God had been good to her. A time shortly before her son had been born, when Sarah's jealousy was just beginning to brew. A time when she had fled, afraid of Sarah's evil temper.

Then God had sent an angel to comfort her. "Call your son Ishmael," the angel had told her. "The name means 'God has heard'."

Ishmael was moaning. She could hear him crying out in his sleep. Would his name hold true? Hagar wondered. Would God hear him now?

One vulture.

At the sound of the boy's cry, the fourth vulture cried back—long and hard and fierce. And instead of descending on their victim, the other three vultures flew away.

Hagar ran to Ishmael, ran to the bush, ran to rescue him from the great dark bird that still remained. She threw herself over her son, wrapped herself around him, buried her head, shut her eyes and waited.

The fourth vulture dropped lower, in ever shrinking circles. It grew larger and larger the closer it got, until it was a huge winged shadow, blocking out the scorching eye of the sun. It hovered over Hagar and Ishmael, hung low in the air. And then the vulture spoke!

"Don't be afraid," it said. "God has heard the cries of your son. See: I have chased away the vultures. I have shielded you from the sun. And now I have something to show you."

Slowly, Hagar lifted her head and looked up.

Round, dark eyes.

Black, feathery hair.

And a sharp beak of a nose.

The face that greeted her looked much like a bird's. But the kindness and love in that face could only have come from somewhere far beyond the sky. And she knew in a moment that the wings beating above her were angel wings.

Like a mother cradling twin children, the angel lifted Hagar and Ishmael into its wings. They flew straight for the sun, high above the desert, until they could see for miles in each direction.

The angel turned to the north. "There is Abraham's camp, the place from which you came."

Then it turned to the south. "There is an oasis—with water and food, where you can rest and live!"

Finally, it turned to the east. "And there—do you see it? All that land and the land beyond? That is the land that will one day belong to your son Ishmael and to his sons after him. God has promised."

And then the angel dived straight for the oasis. And the swiftness of the dive startled Hagar, sent her hair whipping around her head, and made her clutch tightly the soft feathers that surrounded her. But even the speed of their descent could not shake the smile that now rested on Hagar's face.

When they reached the shimmering pool, Hagar filled her water pouch until it wanted to burst. Then she poured the water into Ishmael's mouth and over his face, and into her own mouth, too. And when at last she had drunk her fill, she turned to thank the angel.

But it was gone. The sky was empty. The sun had begun to set—no longer the burning eye of an enemy, but the warm, watchful gaze of a friend.

And that's when Hagar gave thanks to God.

For one angel.

One promise.

And no more vultures.

Sometimes it's hard to believe in promises.

But even though Abraham, Sarah and Hagar found it

hard to believe, God kept his promise to them. He gave Abraham and Sarah a son named Isaac. He heard the cries of Hagar's son, rescued him, and made a huge and powerful nation from his descendants. Ishmael's descendants were called Ishmaelites. They lived in the wilderness, hunted their food with bows and arrows, and were often wild and fierce.

You can read the stories of Abraham, Sarah, Isaac, Hagar and Ishmael in the book of Genesis, chapters 12 to 25. But be sure to read to the end. For when Abraham died, Isaac and Ishmael came together to bury him. The man who had almost given up hope in God's promise was laid to rest by, not one, but two sons of promise.

THE DONKEY AND THE SWORD

There were so many things the old donkey wanted to say:

"Could you brush a little harder?"

"Do you mind if we stop and rest now?"

"Barley cakes again?"

So many things. But donkeys were donkeys. And people were people. So she had to rely on sneezing and snorting, bucking and stalling, and the occasional huffy hee-haw, to tell her master what she wanted.

Balaam had been a good master, really. They'd been together since they were boy and foal, dashing around father Beor's yard till the sweat dripped off his forehead and lathered up on her sides.

Who could have guessed that Balaam would grow up to be so important?

He was doing some important thing now—meeting with important people. Well, at least their horses were important. She knew that much. Tall, white stallions pawing the ground not a double donkey's length away from her. Neighing and whinnying to each other in high and horsey tones.

They were obviously not interested in talking with her, so she clip-clopped up to a window to see what her master was doing. There were three other men with him, one for each horse. She couldn't understand what they were saying. But if she could have, she would have known that the men were princes, and she would have heard their very generous offer.

"Balaam, son of Beor," said the first man, "we bring you greetings from the king of Moab. The people of Israel have come into our land, licking up all that is around them like an ox licks up grass. They have already defeated our neighbours, and we fear that they will destroy us next."

"And so we beg you," continued the second man, "to come with us and curse them. For we have heard that you are a great prophet, and whoever you curse stays cursed, and whoever you bless stays blessed."

"Look, here is silver! Here is gold!" said the third man. "And our king promises that you may have whatever else you want, if you will only come and curse these people."

Balaam looked at the three princes, and he looked at the gold. This was not the first time the king of Moab had made such an offer. Each time Balaam had looked to God for advice. And each time, God had plainly told him not to curse the people of Israel. They were special to God.

Still, thought Balaam, all that gold . . . A new house. A new wardrobe. A new horse! His old grey donkey had grown awfully slow. Hmmmm . . . he wondered . . . perhaps God had changed his mind.

"Gentlemen," Balaam announced. "Stay with me tonight. I will speak with God, and in the morning you shall have my decision."

The donkey watched the princes leave her master's room. She watched her master pace the floor. She watched him sit down, lift up his hands and talk to the ceiling. Then she nodded off to sleep, her chin on the windowsill.

As it happened, God was watching Balaam, too. And God could see a battle going on in Balaam's heart—a battle between Balaam's desire to do what was right and his desire for gold. God could also see that Balaam was determined to go with the princes. So God spoke.

"All right, Balaam," he said. "You may go with the princes tomorrow. But you must say only what I tell you. No more. No less."

The next morning Balaam was in a dreadful mood. He had not slept at all well. And the battle was still raging in his heart. The donkey could tell that her master was upset by the way he kept digging his heels into her side and prodding her along. She wanted to tell him that she was moving as fast as she could. She wanted to say that she didn't care about keeping up with those show-off stallions. She wanted to say that years of loyal service were worth far more than a flashy mane and a little extra speed.

But donkeys were donkeys, and people were people. So she just shook her long ears and clip-clopped along at a donkey's pace until the three horses and their princes were almost out of sight. And that's when the battle in Balaam's heart came to an end.

I am a great prophet, he told himself. Whoever I curse stays cursed. Whoever I bless stays blessed. Everyone says so. So why shouldn't I be wearing beautiful clothes? And why shouldn't I be riding a strong stallion—instead of this plodding old donkey?

I will do what the king asks, he decided. I will curse the Israelites. Surely God won't mind, just this once.

But God did mind. For God still had his eye on Balaam's heart, and he could see it sparkle and shine with thoughts of gold. So God sent an angel to warn Balaam and to win back his greedy heart.

The donkey saw the angel right away. It was standing in front of her and blocking the road. It was three donkeys high and two donkeys wide. And it was waving a sword that could chip-chop any clip-clopping creature in half.

She didn't know what this thing was after, and she didn't take time to ask. After all, donkeys were donkeys,

and this thing was ... well, whatever it was, it didn't look happy. So she turned off the road and ran into a vineyard to hide.

Balaam, on the other hand, could not see the angel. And he was angry. First his old donkey couldn't keep up, and now she was dashing off on some detour. "Get back!" he shouted through a mouthful of grape leaves. "Get back on the road!" And he pulled hard on the donkey's reins and kicked even harder into her sides.

This kind of language the donkey understood. But she decided that if there was ever a time for her to be donkey-stubborn, this was it. So she ignored her master's commands and headed for a path at the far end of the vineyard—away from that thing with the sword.

But all of a sudden, the enormous angel was blocking her path once again.

"Stand still, donkey," the angel commanded in a voice that made a hee-haw sound like a whisper. "It's not you I want. It's Balaam, your master." Then it raised the sword as if it was going to strike.

Perhaps the donkey felt a sudden streak of loyalty to her master. Or maybe she was just too terrified to stand still. In any case, when she saw the sword above her head, the old donkey bolted through the narrow gap between the angel and the stone wall of the vineyard.

But in the process, she also managed to crush Balaam's foot against the wall's rough stones. And because Balaam still could not see the angel, he was furious.

"Stupid animal! Worthless beast!" he bellowed.

"Stop!" And he struck her fiercely across the neck.

There was no time to stop, the donkey decided. There was time only to run. And run she did. But the path grew narrower and the walls on either side grew closer. And then the donkey once more found herself face to face with the angel. This time there was no gap to slip through—not so much as a bridle's breadth.

And so the donkey came to a sudden stop and dropped to her knees. Balaam tumbled over her head and landed right at the feet of the angel.

When he reached for his staff, the donkey thought he might—wonder of wonders—fight the enormous thing. What she didn't know was that Balaam still could not see the angel. What she didn't expect was what happened next.

Balaam struck *her* with the staff. Hard and cruel, as he'd never struck her before.

The donkey was hurt and angry. If only she could talk. Now, more than ever before, she wanted her master to know how she felt. But donkeys were donkeys. And people were people. So she sneezed and snorted and shook her head and got ready to let out the loudest, angriest hee-haw she knew. But when she opened her mouth, this came out instead:

"What have I done to you to make you hit me?"

"What have you done?" Balaam spluttered and roared. "You've made me look like a fool in front of some very important people—that's what. And you've probably broken my foot as well. And if I could afford a

sword instead of this ridiculous staff, I'd kill you here and now."

"Kill me?" howled the donkey. "But why? We've been together all these years. We've shared roads and deserts and mountains and streams. And in all those miles, have I ever let you down?"

"Well . . . no," huffed Balaam.

And then he stopped. And he stared at his donkey. And his donkey stared back.

And no words, donkey or human, could describe their expressions or express the surprise they felt.

"We're talking!" said the donkey. "But that can't be. After all, donkeys are donkeys, and people are people."

"And sometimes people are donkeys, too," said another voice—a deep, rumbling voice.

It was the angel with the sword. The angel the donkey had seen all along. The angel that Balaam could finally see, too. And both the donkey and Balaam fell down in terror at the angel's feet.

"Take your master Balaam, for example," explained the angel to the donkey. "He decides to do what he knows will displease God. I come to warn him, to frighten him, to stop him from cursing God's people. You do everything you can to save him from my sword, donkey. And what is your reward? The same thanks he gives to his God—abuse and scorn. He's a stubborn man, your master. More stubborn than any donkey."

"I—I am sorry now," Balaam stammered. "I didn't see you . . . didn't know you were there." His voice was little more than a whisper. "And if you want me to, I'll go back home right away."

The angel lowered its sword and shook its head. "No, Balaam. God wants you to go with the princes. He has a surprise for the king of Moab. But you must do as God commanded—say only what he tells you to say. No more. And no less."

And then, before the angel disappeared, it waved the sword over Balaam's head one last time, just to make sure he got the point.

Balaam climbed aboard his donkey. As best they could, they raced after the princes, catching them finally as night fell. When they met the king of Moab, Balaam remembered to do exactly what God had commanded him. Every time the king asked Balaam to curse the people of Israel, God whispered a blessing from him to say instead. And since everybody knows that what Balaam blesses stays blessed, the people of

Israel enjoyed happiness and prosperity for a long, long time.

The king was furious, of course. In fact, Balaam was lucky to return home with his life—much less any gold or silver.

As for the donkey, she never spoke again. But then, she never felt the need to. For, from that time on, Balaam could not have been a more grateful or caring master.

After all, donkeys are donkeys. And people are people. And as long as they understand each other, there isn't much left to say.

The Bible never has another good word to say about Balaam, even though he did end up blessing God's people.

Balaam began his blessings by calling himself "the man whose eyes are opened". The problem was, Balaam's eyes didn't stay open for very long. In no time we find him once again hooked up with the king of Moab, this time encouraging God's people to worship false gods. It's not surprising, therefore, that another book in the Bible—Joshua—lists Balaam's name among the enemies who were killed when God's people finally entered the promised land of Canaan.

I'd like to think that the donkey was somewhere else when Balaam was killed. Off in the fields, maybe, munching a weed and shaking her shaggy head at what a donkey her master had become. You can read the story of Balaam in the book of Numbers, chapters 22 to 24.

ANGEL FOOD

Elijah was a pretty good prophet.

With God's help, he raised a boy from the dead. With God's help, he stopped the rain from falling, as a warning to Israel's evil King Ahab. And with God's help, he defeated the false priests of the even-more-evil Queen Jezebel.

So what was he doing sitting under a bush in the middle of the desert?

He was thinking about giving up, that's what.

He was tired—tired of fighting the evil in his land, and then seeing it all come back again. He was afraid—afraid that Queen Jezebel would carry out her threat to track him down and kill him. And he was worried—worried that even God would not be able to help him this time. Worried enough to run and hide in the desert.

And so Elijah prayed a prayer, a sad and tired and frustrated prayer. "Take me away, God," he prayed.

"Take my life before Jezebel does. Kill me now. I've had enough."

And then, with a bush for his blanket and a desert stone for his pillow, Elijah fell into an exhausted sleep.

God heard Elijah's prayer. God understood Elijah's fear and frustration. So God answered Elijah.

Down the secret stairs from heaven, where God's surprises are stored, came an angel. A very special angel. An angel who was more like your mother than your father. An angel who was more of a "she" than a "he".

The angel pulled back a branch of the bush that covered Elijah and let one or two sunbeams land on the prophet's sleeping face. "Poor tired thing," she whispered. And she gently shook her angel head. Then she let go of the branch and rubbed her big hands together as if she was ready to get to work.

The angel reached into one big apron pocket and pulled out a flat spoon. From her other pocket, she fetched a deep, wide, wooden bowl. She set these

down beside the sleeping prophet and whispered softly in his ear, "Be back in a minute, pet. I've got some shopping to do."

Then she threw herself into the sky and flew north, straight for the fertile lands along the Jordan River.

The angel stopped at a threshing floor and swept a pile of freshly harvested wheat into her apron pocket. Next, she swooped low over an orchard and snatched a branch, heavy with fresh fruit, from an olive tree. Finally, the angel soared high into the hills above the river and scooped a cup of fresh, cool water from a mountain stream. Then she sailed back to Elijah—without dropping a seed or spilling a drop.

The prophet turned and shook and mumbled in his sleep.

"Just rest now, my dear," the angel whispered. "It won't be long." And then she began to hum. (A hymn from Heaven's Throne Room? A ditty from Heaven's Kitchen? Or maybe they were one and the same.)

She hummed as she dumped the wheat—kafloosh!—onto a flat desert rock and ground it into flour. She hummed as she clutched the olives in her big angel hand and—squooge!—crushed the oil out of them. She hummed as she mixed the oil and the flour together in the bowl and—bloop!—added just one long drop of the mountain water.

And then she stopped humming. And stood up. And snapped her fingers.

Eggs!

She knew she'd forgotten something. Not even an angel can make cake without eggs.

The angel wiped her hands on her apron and cocked her head, listening to the sounds of the desert. She heard the desert wind pick up bits of sand and send them scraping against desert stones. She heard tiny desert animals skitter and slither and skip across the desert floor.

And then she heard what she was listening for—the soft, chirping song of a desert bird. A partridge.

Quick as a bird herself, the angel chased the sound and found a nest. She whispered something to the partridge, who bowed and stepped aside. And the angel bent down and listened to the nest. In two of the eggs, she heard the flutter and scratch of young bird life. But two were silent and would never be more than eggs. Those she took, with a grateful nod to the mother. Then she flew back to Elijah.

The angel mixed in the eggs and whipped up the batter until it was rich and creamy and thick. And, as a final touch, she reached into her pocket and pulled out a tiny bottle of... Something. (A spice from Heaven's Kitchen? A gift from Heaven's Throne Room? Or maybe they were one and the same.) She opened the bottle and sprinkled exactly seven golden flakes into the batter. Then she dipped one finger into the mix and tasted to make sure it was just right.

Finally, she reached down deep into the hot desert sand. Down, down, down—until she found a steaming hot rock at the bottom of a boiling underground stream. She grabbed hold of that rock and yanked it right out of the ground. Then she carved a hole out of the middle of the rock and poured her batter in. Right away it started to bubble and sizzle and bake.

In no time at all, the cake was done. The angel peeled away the rocky oven as if it was the skin of an orange. Then she set the hot cake and a cup of cold mountain water by Elijah's sleepy head.

She tapped him lightly on the shoulder. "Elijah," she whispered. "Elijah, it's time to wake up."

The last time Elijah had heard those words, they were on his mother's lips. And if his aching body hadn't told him he was lying on the ground in the middle of a desert, he would have sworn he was back at home. So who woke him up? And what was that incredible smell?

Elijah's eyes snapped open, and his questions were answered in a glance. In front of him was a freshly baked cake, a cup of cool water—and an angel!

"Go on," coaxed the smiling angel. "I made it just for you. Try some."

Elijah knew he should be afraid. But he wasn't. What he was—was hungry! He tore off a chunk of the cake and gobbled it down. It was heavenly! Rich but not sickening. Moist but not soggy. Filling but not fattening. So delicious that Elijah had to help himself to another piece. And then another. He would have finished the whole cake if the angel hadn't started

humming her little tune again, and if he hadn't stretched out, tummy full, and fallen asleep all over again. And not a restless sleep this time, but a long and dreamy snooze.

Quietly the angel tidied up her utensils, tucking them one by one into her pockets. And when Elijah had slept long enough, she tapped him on the shoulder again. "Wake up, Elijah. Finish the cake. You have a long trip ahead of you. You need all the strength you can get."

Again Elijah opened his eyes. The cake was still there. But this time the angel was gone. (Gone to Heaven's Throne Room? Back to Heaven's Kitchen? Or maybe they are one and the same.)

Elijah quickly finished off the cake, licking his fingers and picking up each crumb. When he was done, he was different. He was no longer tired. The sleep had refreshed him, and the cake had filled him up so he felt as if he could walk for forty days if he had to.

And he was no longer worried or afraid. Let Jezebel come! Let Ahab do his worst! God would take care of his prophet. Elijah was sure of that now.

That very moment, Elijah stood up and set off for Mount Horeb, the holy mountain. He was going to meet God there. He was going to find out what God wanted him to do next. And he was going to thank God for answering his prayer in a way he'd never expected— with a cup of cold mountain water and an angel food cake.

The story of the angel who fed Elijah is found in chapter 18 of 1 Kings. Later in that chapter, we discover what happened after Elijah ate the angel's cake and walked for forty days to Mount Horeb.

Huddled in a cave high up on the mountain, Elijah waited for God. First a powerful wind blew by, tearing the rocks off the mountainside. But God was not in the wind.

Then an earthquake rumbled and shook the mountain. But God was not in the earthquake.

Next, flames of a mighty fire crackled and roared past Elijah. But God was not in the fire.

Finally, Elijah heard another sound. No more than a whisper, really. And—surprise!—this time it was God. In this still, small voice, God spoke to his discouraged prophet, comforted him, and sent him back to work.

Surprises. This chapter in the Bible is full of them—an angel chef, a miracle cake, and a great big God with a quiet little voice.

THE MEN WHO
LIKED TO SAY NO

When they lived in Jerusalem, their Hebrew friends knew them as Hannaniah, Mishael and Azariah. When Jerusalem was conquered by Babylon and they were taken captive to the palace of King Nebuchadnezzar, they were given Babylonian names. Then everyone knew them as Shadrach, Meshach, and Abednego.

But anyone who knew them well, knew them as The Men Who Liked to Say No.

They were handsome, these young men. And clever and strong, as well. Sons of Jerusalem's most important families. So Nebuchadnezzar treated them well—gave them soft beds to sleep on, the finest food to eat, an education at his very best university and, when they graduated, important jobs in his government. He hoped that they would forget about Jerusalem and learn to call Babylon home.

But Nebuchadnezzar hadn't reckoned on them being The Men Who Liked to Say No.

King Nebuchadnezzar's herald was a tiny man with enormous lungs. His name, Shamashumukin, was equally enormous. But anyone who knew him well, knew him as The Man Who Liked to Say Far Too Much.

One day Shamashumukin made an important announcement:

"All prefects and satraps,
All magistrates and judges,
All counsellors and governors,
All big shots and hobnobs,
Must report to the Plain of Dura, outside the city.
King Nebuchadnezzar has a surprise for you."

When the officials got there, they found a golden statue—an idol nine feet wide and ninety feet tall. It was the biggest statue they had ever seen. And gathered around the statue was the biggest band they had ever heard.

Shamashumukin cleared his throat loudly and took a deep, long breath.

"Hear me,
People of all nations and stations and languages,
People of all places and races and climes,
People of all landscapes and body shapes and backgrounds,
People of all time zones and hormones and kinds.

"At the sound of
  The trumpet, the trigon, the horn and the bagpipe,
  The oboe, the zither, the harp and the lyre,
  The wahoo, the farney, the honk and the oompah,
  All of you must bow down and worship this
golden statue.

  "And anyone who does not, will be thrown into a
  Hot and horrible,
  Bright and blazing,
  Flaming, fiery furnace!"

While Shamashumukin caught his breath, King Nebuchadnezzar gave the signal and the band began to play. At once, everyone fell down and worshipped the statue.

Well, almost everyone.

There were three officials way at the back who did not bow down and worship the statue: Shadrach, Meshach, and Abednego—The Men Who Liked to Say No.

Now, most people knew Nebuchadnezzar as the great and powerful ruler of Babylon (not to mention most of the rest of the world).

But anyone who knew him well, knew him as The King Who Liked to Say GRRRR.

And when he saw the three men standing when they should have been bowing, that is exactly what King

Nebuchadnezzar said.

"GRRRR," he snarled. "Who dares defy my order?"

"GRRRR," he growled. "Who dares insult my god?"

"GRRRR," he roared. "Who dares? Who dares?"

As it happened, there were several big shots and hobnobs nearby who knew who dared. These men were native Babylonians who didn't much like these foreigners from Jerusalem having such important jobs.

"Their names are Shadrach, Meshach and Abednego," they said.

"GRRRR," the king snarled. "Bring them to me at once!"

Immediately, The Men Who Liked to Say No were brought before Nebuchadnezzar.

"Well," demanded the king. "You heard the order, and you failed to obey. What do you have to say for yourselves?"

"No," said Shadrach. "We will not worship your statue."

"No," said Meshach. "Our God has told us that such worship would be wrong."

"No," said Abednego. "We will not forget our God or his Law or the wonderful land he gave us—the land from which our people were taken."

The king shook with rage. He could hardly control himself. "GRRRR," he growled once more. "Perhaps you did not hear what would happen if you disobeyed."

The herald took a quick breath and repeated himself: "Anyone who disobeys will be thrown into a

Hot and horrible,

Bright and blazing,

Flaming, fiery furnace!"

"Is that what you want?" snapped the king.

"No," said Shadrach. "But we will not worship your golden statue."

"No," said Meshach. "But we will not forget our God."

"No," said Abednego. "And we know that he will not forget us."

"THEN OFF TO THE FURNACE!" roared the king.

"Make it hot!" Nebuchadnezzar growled at his herald. "Two, four, six, seven times hotter than it's ever been before. And tie them up tight, so there is no chance for escape."

And so, tightly bound, The Men Who Liked to Say No were thrown into the furnace by three of the king's bravest guards. The flames were so hot and the heat so fierce that the guards died immediately.

"Charred. Sizzled. Burned to a crisp," noted the herald.

Things were different, however, for The Men Who Liked to Say No.

They looked at each other. They weren't burning. They weren't boiling. They weren't even sweating.

And they weren't alone.

They could barely make him out, moving through the fire. A flash of orange hair. Flaming red fingers. And a pair of burning eyes. He might have been called The Angel Who Danced in Fire. But anyone who knew him well, knew him as The Angel Who Liked to Say God Is with You.

He flickered like the flames before them—now crimson and orange, now yellow and gold, now blue and white. One after another, the angel touched a finger to the ropes that bound each man. The ropes smoked and sizzled and then burned through. But there was not so much as a blister on the skin of Shadrach, Meshach and Abednego.

Then the angel spoke, and his voice roared and rumbled like a furnace. "God Is with You!" he said. And the fire flickered and trembled in reply. The angel's eyes glowed bright with joy as they moved from Shadrach to Meshach to Abednego. "God Is with You!" he said again, his voice crackling and sparking with delight. "Have no fear."

A smile ignited on one cheek and burned like a fuse across the angel's face. He took Shadrach's hand and led the three men in a circle dance through the fiery furnace. They shuffled their feet through the white hot coals. They ran their hands along the red hot walls. They filled their lungs with the black, hot air of the furnace. And they blew out fat, round smoke rings.

Meanwhile, outside the furnace, Nebuchadnezzar's lips were no longer twisted in an angry snarl. They hung open and limp with amazement. "I thought we threw three men into the furnace," he said. "But, look, there are four men in there now."

Shamashumukin crept closer and looked. Then he turned to the king, his face red from the heat and dripping with sweat. "It is an angel, your majesty. A creature from heaven. Perhaps even the very God whom Shadrach, Meshach and Abednego refused to forget. If so, he is a powerful God indeed. They are unharmed!"

Nebuchadnezzar leaped to his feet and called for

Shadrach, Meshach and Abednego to come out.

The three men waded through the flames to the mouth of the furnace, kicking coals as they went. When they turned to thank the angel, he smiled and changed to smoke in Shadrach's hand, leaving behind a whisper that curled gently up around their heads.

"Don't forget," said the whisper, "God Is with You."

As soon as the men stepped out of the furnace, the king's officials gathered round to have a closer look.

The satraps and prefects inspected them carefully. "Not a trace of smoke," they noted.

The counsellors and governors smelled their clothes. "Fresh as a Babylonian spring," they observed.

The big shots and hobnobs touched their hair. "Not even singed!" they cried.

Finally, Nebuchadnezzar himself spoke up. "Praise be to the God of Shadrach, Meshach and Abednego— the supreme God! They did not forget him, and he did not forget them, but sent his angel to save them. I therefore order that, from now on, no one shall say anything bad about this God. And if anyone does," he added—just for growling's sake—"he shall be . . ."

"Torn from limb to limb?" suggested Shamashumukin. "Chopped into a million pieces? Separated from all his bodily parts?"

"Yes, yes!" agreed the king. "And what is more, I shall promote Shadrach, Meshach and Abednego to

even higher positions in my kingdom."

Then he looked squarely at The Men Who Liked to Say No. "Surely you can say yes to that?"

Shadrach looked at Meshach. Meshach looked at Abednego. Abednego looked at Shadrach. Then, together, they looked at the king.

"No problem!" they said.

The Babylonians were not only powerful, they were also crafty. Whenever they conquered a nation, they carried off the children of that nation's most important families and raised them in Babylon.

They hoped that as those children grew up, they would come to realize that the Babylonian way of life was good and then help the rest of their people enjoy being part of the Babylonian empire.

That is what happened to the Hebrew boys Shadrach, Meshach and Abednego (and to their friend Daniel, whom you will meet in the next story). The problem was that, from the start, these four boys were convinced that the Babylonian ways were nothing like as good as the ways of their own people and, more importantly, the ways of their God.

So, long before they were The Men Who Liked to Say No (in chapter 3 of the book of Daniel*), Shadrach, Meshach, Abednego and Daniel were The Boys Who Liked to Say No.*

Sometimes you have to stand up for what you believe in, even if that is dangerous or embarrassing or means saying

No when everyone else thinks there's nothing wrong with saying Yes. You may feel as if you're standing in a lonely place at the time. But as Shadrach, Meshach and Abednego discovered, that place is often where God's angels are standing, too.

DINNER IN THE LIONS' DEN

King Darius did not want to dump Daniel into the lions' den. And Daniel certainly did not want to be dumped there. But a law was a law—even if the king had been tricked into making it. And Daniel had broken the law by praying to God when the law said he shouldn't.

While Daniel's enemies were laughing and slapping each other on the back for tricking the king, two things happened at almost the same time.

King Darius sent up a prayer, like a small white bird, to ask Daniel's God to protect Daniel.

And Daniel sent up a small white bird of his own.

It did not take long for God to send an answer back. But it might have seemed long to Daniel as he was lowered into the lions' den.

There were four lions in the den. A huge father lion

with a shaggy brown mane. A sleek mother lion with golden brown hair. And two tumbling and not quite grown-up cubs.

The lions looked at Daniel and drooled. Their bellies growled as only lion bellies can.

"He's skinny," said Father Lion, "and scrawny and old."

"He'll be tough," said Mother Lion, "but tasty."

"Dibs on the drumsticks!" said one of the cubs.

When Daniel looked at the lions, all he saw were four open mouths and four sets of sharp, white teeth. And all Daniel heard was a rising, roaring chorus as the lions padded closer.

Suddenly, something like a curtain seemed to open between heaven and earth. "Wait just a minute!" called a voice through the opening. God's answer had arrived.

It was an angel. An angel who was good with lions. An angel who looked a bit like a lion himself. A great, stocky, slab-footed angel with hulking hands and a shaggy brown head of hair.

"It's not time for that yet," called the angel.

"Oh?" growled Father Lion. "Then what time is it, Mr Angel?"

The angel paused for a moment and thought. "It's scratching time," he said.

Then the angel laid one huge hand on Father Lion's head and started scratching behind his ears. Those chunky fingers felt good, and Father Lion stopped his growling, laid himself down and began to purr. With his other hand, the angel scratched Mother Lion at the base of her neck where it met her shoulders. Soon she was purring, too.

"Me next! Me next!" shouted the cubs. And for a long time, Daniel heard nothing but scratching and purring and mewing.

Then one of the lions' tummies started to growl again. And Father Lion glanced at Daniel through his mane, rolled his tongue out across his lips and showed the end of one white fang.

"What time is it now, Mr Angel?" he asked.

"It's belly-rubbing time, of course," answered the angel.

Father Lion muttered a disappointed "Oh," but the other members of his family were quite excited.

"Me first!" mewed one of the cubs.

"You were first last time," mewed the other.

"There'll be turns for everyone," said the angel as he turned over a cub with each hand. Then he smiled at Daniel and winked.

And then . . . you know how it is with belly rubbing. First you're rubbing bellies and then you're wrestling. If any of Daniel's enemies had found the courage to put his ear to the stone on top of the den, he would have thought that old Daniel was being torn to pieces. But it was only the lions rolling and biting and pawing at each other as they played "Trap the Tail" and "Cuff the Cub." And that great, tawny angel was playing hardest of all.

When they had finished, the lions collapsed, exhausted, on the floor of their den.

"What time is it? What time is is now, Mr Angel?" yawned Father Lion.

The angel stretched wide his arms, shook his shaggy head and yawned back, "It's sleepy time, I think."

And the lions curled up like housecats in front of a fire and were soon fast asleep. The angel curled up with them, wrapping his long, lion-like self around them. But he kept one eye open, just in case.

Next morning everyone in the den was awakened by the crunching, scraping sound of the stone den cover being hastily slid aside.

"Daniel!" The king's voice echoed through the den.

"Daniel! Has your God answered my prayer? Has your God saved you?"

"Yes, your majesty, he has indeed." Daniel's sleepy voice bounced back up into the light. "God has answered both our prayers. He sent his angel to shut the lions' mouths."

The delighted king had his servants quickly pull Daniel out of the den. Then they dropped Daniel's enemies—those laughing, back-slapping tricksters—into the den instead.

The lions stretched and stood up and stared. They were wide awake now. And very hungry.

The angel stretched and stood up with them. "Well, I must go now," he said. "Goodbye, lions."

And then he pulled back that mysterious curtain between heaven and earth and started to step inside.

"Wait!" growled Father Lion. "Before you go . . . tell me, Mr Angel, what time is it now?"

The angel looked at Daniel's enemies and the four hungry lions. And he grinned a wide cat grin. Then he drew the curtain around him, leaving only his answer and a shadow of that grin behind.

"What time is it?" said the angel. "It's dinner time."

The story of Daniel and the lions is found in chapter 6 of the book of Daniel. *This book has lots of exciting stories about what happened to God's people, the Hebrews, when they were captives in the land of Babylon.*

When Daniel was an old man, the Babylonians were conquered by the Persians. The Persian Empire was huge. It included many nations, each of which had its own gods or goddesses. As ruler of the empire, King Darius must have known about many gods and goddesses. But when he saw what happened to Daniel in the lions' den, Darius discovered something special about the God that Daniel worshipped.

After Daniel was safely away from the lions, the king sent a letter to all nations in his empire, encouraging everyone to worship the "living God" of Daniel. You can read his letter for yourself in verses 25-27 of Daniel 6.

$\mathcal{T}$HE SURPRISE

The angel Gabriel sat in the corner and watched.

The girl was only thirteen. Fourteen, at most. Barely a woman, by the shape of her. With long, dark hair and bright olive skin. Not beautiful, but far from plain. Pretty.

The last thing he wanted to do was scare her. Like he'd scared that old priest Zechariah.

You did everything possible to ease the shock, Gabriel assured himself. No blinding flashes of light. No angelic choirs. You just appeared to him there beside the altar. He was in the temple, for heaven's sake! What better place to meet an angel?

But the old man had still been spooked. He clutched at his heart. He wobbled and shook like the smoke curling up from the altar.

"Don't be afraid," Gabriel had said. "The news I

have for you is good. Your wife will have a baby. You will call him John. He will prepare God's people to meet the Messiah."

The announcement was nothing like he'd practised it, of course. He'd had to blurt it out all in one breath because the old man looked like he was about to keel over.

Gabriel hugged his knees and scrunched himself back into the corner. He hated these surprise visits, and that's all there was to it.

The girl was whistling now. Doing her ordinary, everyday chores—as if this was some ordinary everyday, and not the most extraordinary day of her life.

The angel rested his chin on his knees. Think, Gabriel, think, he muttered to himself. She's young. But she's probably fragile like that old priest. So how do you do it? How do you tell her that God is about to change her whole life, without scaring her to death?

Mary began to sweep as she whistled. And as the dust motes danced in front of her broom, catching the sun and changing shape like dirty little clouds, Gabriel had an idea.

What about a vision? he asked himself. It always worked with the prophets. The dust rises and takes on the form of a man. "Mary," the dust-man says, "you are going to be the mother of the Son of God!"

Gabriel shook his head, then buried it in his arms. No, no, no, he decided. Still too spooky. And besides, all it takes is a strong breeze and the poor girl has to dust her house all over again!

It was too late now, anyway. Mary had put her broom away and was across the room preparing dinner. Gabriel climbed up out of the corner and stretched. Then he followed her to the table.

Bread. She was making bread. And as she mixed the ingredients, another idea started to knead itself together and rise in Gabriel's head.

He could write the message in the flour on the table. Of course! An invisible hand, like the one that scratched those letters on the wall in Babylon. But it would have

to be brief. It was a small table, after all. And there wasn't much time. Mary's parents were both gone, and there was no telling when they would be back. He wouldn't want to be surprised in the middle of his message. Gabriel hated surprises!

And then somebody knocked on the door. Gabriel jumped, startled by the sound. Mary quietly turned and walked to the door, wiping her hands as she went. It was a girl about Mary's age. Gabriel watched as they hugged and exchanged greetings. She had a brief message for Mary.

It wasn't long before Mary said goodbye and shut the door again.

I could do that, Gabriel thought. Knock at the door, like some unexpected visitor, and just give her the message . . . But what if she got scared and slammed the door in my face? Or what if someone passed by and saw us? She'll have enough explaining to do when the baby comes. She won't need to make excuses for some mysterious stranger.

And then Gabriel sighed. A long, frustrated angel sigh. Gabriel had run out of ideas. Gabriel was running out of time. So Gabriel sighed.

Perhaps it was the sigh. Perhaps it was something else that Mary heard. For whatever reason, she spun around and seemed to hang suspended in the air for a second— like one of those dust motes—her hair flung out behind her, her feet barely touching the floor. And her eyes. Her eyes looked right into Gabriel's.

He hadn't noticed her eyes before. Brown, shining eyes. Young and alive. They should have looked right through him, but they didn't. They stopped where he stood, and they touched him. Somehow she could see him. Somehow she knew he was there.

"Hello, Mary," he said finally, because there was nothing else to say. "God is with you, and wants to do something very special for you."

Mary didn't say anything. But she didn't faint either. And that was a great relief to the angel. She just stood there, shaking ever so slightly, and stared at her guest. He could see those eyes swallow up his words, see the questions and concern in those eyes as the girl tried to puzzle out the meaning of his greeting.

"There's no need to be afraid," Gabriel assured her, although it was hard to know exactly what she was feeling. Was she trembling with fear? Or was it more like excitement? Gabriel couldn't tell. And he didn't like that one bit. This girl was nothing like what he had expected. This girl was a bit of a surprise.

"Look," he continued, "God is very pleased with you. So pleased, in fact, that he wants you to be the mother of a very special child—Jesus, the Messiah. The Deliverer whom your people have been waiting for all these years."

Surely this would shock her, Gabriel thought. And he was ready to catch her if she should fall. But all she did was sit herself down to think. She played with the hem of her dress, folding and unfolding it. She twisted her hair.

Say something, thought Gabriel. Say anything!
And finally she did.

"I don't understand," she said. "How can this happen? How can I become someone's mother when I'm not yet someone's wife?"

This was the last question the angel expected. This girl wasn't hysterical or alarmed. Her question was plain, straightforward and practical.

Gabriel cleared his throat and answered the question as best he could. "The Holy Spirit will visit you. You will be wrapped in the power of the Almighty. And you will give birth to the Son of God."

Mary had never heard of such a thing. And it showed. In her bright brown eyes it showed.

"Listen," Gabriel explained, "God can do anything. Think about your cousin Elizabeth. Well past child-bearing age. Barren, by all accounts. And yet she's expecting a son!"

Mary looked up at the angel and shook her head. She was still trying to take it in. But she wasn't afraid, he could tell that much. She was strong, this girl. A doer. A coper. A fighter. And when she finally weighed it all, Gabriel knew what her answer would be even before she gave it. Those eyes of hers were shining fierce and bold.

"I'll do it," she said. "I'll do it. I will be whatever God wants me to be."

Gabriel nodded. Then he turned to leave. He reached out to open the curtain—the curtain between heaven and earth—and saw that his hand was trembling.

He turned back to look at Mary one last time. And in the mirror of her eyes, Gabriel saw a shocked angel face.

Mary smiled at him.

He smiled back. Perhaps surprises aren't so bad after all, he thought.

Then Gabriel pulled the curtain behind him and said goodbye to the girl. The girl who had surprised an angel. And who would one day surprise the world.

When the Gospel writer Luke *tells his story about Jesus' life, he gives extra attention to the women who played an important part in that life. Mary, whose meeting with Gabriel is described in chapter 1 of Luke, is at the top of his list.*

It has been suggested that, as Luke did research and fact-finding for his book, he had the chance to actually talk with Mary—to hear, firsthand, her side of the story. As a result, Luke may have seen more fully what Gabriel only glimpsed: one surprising, remarkable woman.

People are often like that. Ordinary, everyday-looking people turn out to be surprises because of the love or the patience or the forgiveness they show us. Such people are gifts to us, I think. Like Mary was. Surprises so wonderful, so unexpected that they sometimes catch even angels off guard.

A NIGHT THE STARS
DANCED FOR JOY

The old shepherd,
  the shepherd's wife
  and the shepherd boy
lay on their backs on top of the hill.

Their hands were folded behind their heads, and
their feet stretched out in three directions like points
on a compass. Their day's work was done. Their sheep
had dropped off to sleep. And they had run out of things
to say.

So they just lay there on top of that hill and stared
lazily into the night sky.

It was a clear night. There were no clouds for shy
stars to hide behind. And the bolder stars? For some
reason, they seemed to be shining more proudly than
even the old shepherd could remember.

Suddenly, what must have been the boldest star of all

came rushing across the sky, dancing from one horizon to the other and showing off its sparkling serpent's tail.

"Shooting star," said the boy dreamily. "Make a wish."

The old shepherd and his wife said nothing. They were too old for games and too tired tonight, even to say so.

But they were not too old for wishing.

The old shepherd fixed his eyes on a cluster of stars that looked like a great bear. And he thought about the cluster of scars on his leg—jagged reminders of a battle he'd fought with a real bear long ago. A battle to save his sheep. He had been young and strong then. He'd won that battle.

There were other scars, too, mapped out like a hundred roads across his back. Souvenirs of his battles with that Great Bear, Rome. The land of Israel belonged to his people, not to the Roman invaders who were devouring it with their tyranny and taxes. So why should he bow politely to Roman soldiers and surrender his sheep for their banquets? Greedy tyrants. Uniformed thieves. That's what they were—the lot of them. And even their claw-sharp whips would not change his mind.

And so, even though he said nothing, the old shepherd made a wish. He wished for someone to save him. From violence. From greed. From bears.

The shepherd's wife had her eyes shut. This was the hardest time of the day for her. The time when there was nothing to do but try to fall asleep. The time when the wind always carried voices back to her. Her voice and her mother's. Angry, bitter voices. Voices hurling words that hurt. Words she wished she'd never spoken. Words she couldn't take back now, because her mother was dead. And there was no chance to say she was sorry.

And so, even though she said nothing, the shepherd's wife silently wished for peace, for an end to those bitter voices on the wind.

The shepherd boy grew tired of waiting. "All right," he said finally. "*I'll* make a wish then. I wish... I wish... I wish something interesting would happen for a change. Something exciting. I'm tired of just sitting on this hill night after night. I want something to laugh about. To sing and dance about."

The old shepherd turned to look at his wife.

The shepherd's wife opened her eyes and shook her head.

But before either of them could lecture their son about being satisfied with what he had, something happened. Something that suggested the shepherd boy just might get his wish.

Like tiny white buds blossoming into gold flowers, the stars began to swell and spread, until their edges bled together and the sky was filled with a glowing blanket of light. And then that blanket of light began to shrink and gather itself into a brilliant, blinding ball that hung above the shepherds and left the rest of the sky black and empty.

Wide-eyed and slack-jawed, the shepherds dared not move. The wind had stopped. And the shepherds lay glued to the hillside, staring into that light. They watched it slowly change again. Shining rays stretched into arms. Legs kicked out like white beams. And a glowing face blinked bright and burning. The light sprouted wings. It took the shape of an angel. And it spoke.

"Don't be afraid," the angel said. "But sing and dance for joy! I have good news for you. Today, in Bethlehem, your Saviour was born—the special one whom God promised to send you. Here's the proof: if you go to Bethlehem, you will find the baby wrapped in cloths and lying in a feed trough."

The shepherds were still too shocked to speak. But that didn't keep them from thinking.

"Don't be afraid?" thought the old shepherd. "He's got to be kidding."

A baby in a feed trough?" thought the shepherd's wife. "Why even our own son got better treatment than that."

"Sing and dance for joy?" thought the shepherd boy. "Now that's more like it!"

And, as if in answer to the boy's thought, the angel threw his arms and legs wide, like the first step in some heavenly jig. But instead, he flung himself—could it be?—into a thousand different pieces of light, pieces that scattered themselves across the dark blue of the night and landed where the stars had been. Pieces that turned into angels themselves, singing a song that the shepherds had never heard before, to a tune that had been humming in their heads for ever.

"Glory to God in the highest!" the angels sang. "And peace on earth to all."

Some plucked at lyres. Some blew trumpets. Some beat drums. Some banged cymbals. There were dancers, as well—spinning and whirling, larking and leaping across the face of the midnight moon.

Finally, when the music could get no louder, when the singers could sing no stronger, when the dancers could leap no higher, when the shepherds' mouths and eyes could open no further, everything came to a stop.

As quickly as the angels had come, they were gone.

The sky was silent and filled once more with twinkling stars. The shepherds lay there for a moment, blinking and rubbing their eyes.

At last the old shepherd struggled to his feet. "Well," he said, "Looks like we'd better find this baby."

The shepherd's wife pulled herself up, shook the grass off her robe and ran her fingers absently through her hair.

The shepherd boy leaped eagerly to his feet and shouted "Hooray!"

When they got to Bethlehem, things were just as the angel had said. A husband and a young mother. And a baby in a feed trough. A family much like the shepherd's, in fact. Was it possible, the old man wondered, for one so small, so poor, so ordinary, to the be the Saviour? The Promised One?

Then he told the young mother about the angels. And that's when he knew. It was the look in her eyes. The look that said, "How wonderful!" but also, "I'm not surprised." There was something special going on here. The angels knew it. The mother knew it. And now the shepherd and his family knew it, too.

"Well," said the boy as they made their way back to the hill, "my wish came true. Too bad you didn't make a wish."

The old shepherd said nothing. But he ran one finger gently along his scars. Was he imagining things, or were they smaller now?

The shepherd's wife said nothing. She was listening. There were no bitter voices on the wind now. There were songs—heaven songs—and the cry of a newborn child.

"Glory to God in the highest!" she shouted suddenly.

"And peace to everyone on earth!" the old shepherd shouted back.

Then the shepherd boy shouted, too—"Hooray!"—and danced like an angel for joy.

Do Christmas wishes come true? they did for the shepherd boy. In the second chapter of Luke *you can read the original account of that angel visit.*

But what about the old shepherd's wish for someone to save him from the bears of violence and greed? When the baby in the feed trough grew up, he talked about loving others as you want to be loved. He taught that there are more important things than getting as much money as you can. And a lot of violent and greedy people listened to what he said and changed their ways.

And how about the shepherd's wife and her wish for peace? Jesus made that wish come true as well. He explained to people how important it was to forgive those who hurt you. And when he died on the cross for all the wrong and hurtful things other people had done, he made God's own forgiveness available to women and men and children of all times.

ANGEL OF DEATH AND LIFE

The angel sat in the dark and waited.

This was the most unusual assignment he had ever received. Up till now, his missions had always been straightforward—keeping children from falling into wells, helping lost travellers find their way. Typical guardian angel kind of stuff.

But this job was different, very different. A quick beam of light to mark the location, and a strange set of orders that simply said he should wait for his partner to arrive. Partner? He'd never had a partner before. He was big and strong and could do most things on his own. So he couldn't help wondering what this was all about.

And then the angel saw something.

The sun reached one long finger over the horizon and, sure enough, there was someone coming towards him, wading slowly through the darkness as if it were a thick, black sea. Could this be his partner? If so, it was the most unusual angel he had ever seen.

No song. No shimmer. No shine. There was hardly a hint of heaven about him. Instead, he was thin and tired—a small grey mouse of an angel. Barely an angel at all, it seemed.

The first angel raised his hand in a greeting. "Hello," he said. "My name is Candriel. Who are you?"

The second angel sat down beside his partner, but it was a minute or two before he spoke. And when he did, it was in a mouse's whisper that matched his looks.

"My name is Destroyer," he said solemnly. "I am the Angel of Death."

An early morning breeze blew past the angels, but it was not the breeze that made Candriel shiver. He'd heard of this angel. Everyone had. How he'd killed Egyptian first-borns and set God's people free. How he'd slain, single-handed, 185,000 Assyrian soldiers in one night. But to look at him now, sitting there all small and grey and quiet, it hardly seemed possible.

Could this really be the Angel of Death? Candriel wondered. And what kind of mission was this going to be?

"I suppose you have the orders?" said Candriel uncertainly.

The Angel of Death nodded and laid a bony hand on one of his pockets. "I do," he sighed. "But I was told not to open them until we saw women coming up the hill. It's got something to do with a secret—a surprise."

71

A partner. A signal. A surprise. This job gets stranger and stranger, thought Candriel. But all he dared say was, "What do you suppose the orders are?"

The Angel of Death shook his head. "Oh, that's not hard to guess. All you have to do is look around."

The sun's bright scalp edged over the horizon, and Candriel looked. They were in the middle of a grave-yard.

"Death again," Destroyer sighed. "Seems like death is always part of the job for me. So I guess it makes sense that I should play some part in this death, too. The saddest death of all."

Candriel looked again. The sun was a little higher now, and he could see it all clearly. The garden grave-yard. The sleeping soldiers. The city of Jerusalem off in the distance. The huge stone that sealed the tomb beneath them.

"So you've guessed who's in the tomb we're sitting on," said Destroyer.

"Jesus," whispered Candriel. "It's Jesus, isn't it? It's God's Son."

A soldier grunted in his sleep. A bird whistled in the distance. And the Angel of Death just nodded.

"I saw it happen, you know," said Candriel after a while. "I saw him die on the cross. Our whole battalion was ready to burst through the sky, beat the stuffing out of those soldiers, and save him. Uproot that cross, tear it right out of the ground—that's what I would have done. But they wouldn't let us do anything. They said the signal had to come from Him. And the signal never came."

Destroyer turned a grey face to his partner. "I didn't watch," he said softly. "I couldn't. I've seen too much death already. I'm sure He had a reason. He must have. But that didn't make it any easier. Didn't ease the terrible hurt."

"No," agreed Candriel. "He suffered a lot. You could see that. They did some awful things to him."

"That's not what I mean," said Destroyer. "I mean the other kind of hurt that comes with death. Saying goodbye to your friends, to the ones you love. They say that even his mother was there."

Candriel said nothing. He looked puzzled.

"You're a guardian angel, aren't you?" asked

Destroyer. But it wasn't really a question. "Big and strong—the rescuing type."

"Right," said Candriel. "And I'm good at what I do."

"I'm sure you are," said the Angel of Death. "And I'm also sure you feel a lot of joy and gratitude from the people you rescue."

"Oh, yes!" Candriel smiled.

"Well, it's different when you're the Angel of Death. Take the Assyrian army, for example. They had the city of Jerusalem surrounded. They were going to slaughter most of God's people and make slaves of the rest. It was my job to stop them."

"That must have been difficult," Candriel interrupted, "to kill so many of them. I mean, with you being so small."

The Angel of Death looked up at his partner and slowly shook his head. "No," he sighed. "Doing the job was the easy part. A quick breath in the face. That's all it took. Then their eyes glazed over and their hearts grew still.

"The hard part was the thoughts—those thousands and thousands of sad goodbye thoughts:

My wife . . . I'll never see you again.
I'm sorry, Mother. I promised you I would come back.
Grow up well, my son . . . I will miss you.

"Missing. Death is all about missing. That's what I remember most about that night. And that's what I think must have been so hard for Jesus and his friends."

Candriel looked at his partner. And what he saw was sadness. Sadness Like some great thick shell that seemed to crush and shrink Destroyer.

"I just wish," the Angel of Death concluded, "I just wish that once I could have a mission where I remembered not sadness and loss, but the kind of joy and gratitude that you have felt so often."

Candriel didn't know what to say. But he was a guardian angel, after all. So at least he knew what to do. He opened up one shining silver wing, and reaching through the sadness, he wrapped it around the Angel of Death.

They sat there together in the sadness and the new day's light. And then Candriel spotted the women.

"That's the signal," he said. "It's time to read our orders."

The Angel of Death reached into his pocket and handed the scroll to his partner. "You read it," he said.

Candriel took the scroll and started to unroll it. "It's probably very simple," he said. "The women are coming. They're friends of Jesus. We're probably supposed to protect them from these soldiers. It's going to be all right. You'll see."

And then he read the scroll out loud.

"Candriel," the orders said. "Guardian Angel, kind and strong: you wanted so badly to free my Son from his cross. But that was not within your power. What is now within your power is to roll away the stone. Open his tomb and show the world that the one who died on the cross is now alive—free from death for ever! As for you, Destroyer, faithful servant, Angel of Death: someone needs to tell these women that the one they miss is alive. Who better to share this joyful news than one who understands their sadness and loss?"

It took hardly a second. Candriel dropped the orders, leaped off the tomb, and rolled away the stone.

Destroyer was right behind, climbing down after him into the grave. It was empty.

It was empty!

And that's when Candriel saw his partner change.

The soldiers said it was an earthquake. They said they saw a flash of lightning. But Candriel knew different.

The sound that cracked the morning stillness was a sad whisper exploding into a shout of joy. And the light that stunned the soldiers was a grim, grey shadow bursting bright to white.

"He is not here. He is risen! He is alive!" Destroyer shouted to the women.

And the Angel of Death became, forevermore, the Angel of Life.

Angels appear in all four Bible stories about how Jesus rose from the dead. Angels roll away the stone from the

tomb's entrance in Matthew 28. There are angels sitting inside the tomb in the John 20 story. And in Matthew 28, Mark 16 and Luke 24, angels announce that Jesus has risen.

Were any of these the Angel of Death? Nobody knows. The Angel of Death or the Destroyer, as he is sometimes called, appears by name three times in the Bible. But whether he was involved in the Easter story is not certain. I just imagined that his involvement would be a wonderful way to show how Jesus' victory over death might have touched heaven as well as earth.

$\mathscr{A}$ JOKE AT MIDNIGHT

Peter was asleep. His head thrown back, his mouth wide open. Singing a roaring, snoring song.

Peter was asleep, but he wasn't home in bed.

Peter was in prison. Peter the fisherman, the follower and friend of Jesus. There was a guard on his right and a guard on his left. And his arms were chained to the wall.

Peter was dreaming. He dreamed about King Herod who had shut him up in this prison for talking about Jesus. King Herod, who was going to have him killed in the morning.

He dreamed about his friends, who were praying for him at that very moment, praying that he would be set free.

And then he had another dream—a most unusual dream. Peter dreamed he saw a beam of light shoot into his cell, straight down from the ceiling to the floor. And an angel slid down that beam, like a boy shimmying down a tree. The angel was small and slim, no bigger than a boy. And he wore a wide, mischievous grin—as if he was about to play some kind of enormous joke on someone.

Peter wanted to watch, but as so often happens with dreams, he fell back to sleep again. The next thing he knew, someone was thumping him on the side.

Those guards, he thought peevishly. Couldn't they let him have one last night's rest? He turned his head to the left and opened his eyes. The guard was asleep. He turned his head to the right. That guard was asleep, too. Puzzled, he looked straight ahead. And there, not a hand's breadth from his face, was that mischievous grin he'd seen in his dream.

Was Peter dreaming now? He couldn't tell.

The angel wrapped his small hands around two of Peter's fat fisherman fingers and jumped back, pulling Peter to his feet. Then the angel skipped away a few steps and motioned for Peter to shake his hands.

This has got to be a dream, thought Peter. But he shook his hands, like the angel showed him. And his chains fell off!

Quick as a child, the angel leaped to catch them before they rattled to the floor. Then he gently set them down, grinning and giggling all the while.

Peter grinned too. What a dream this is! he thought.

Suddenly, from out of nowhere, Peter's clothes came flying across the cell and hit him smack in the face.

"Put them on," a small voice giggled.

Peter put them on. And just as he'd finished, his sandals dropped lightly—one, two—in front of his feet.

"These, too," the voice giggled again. "It's time to go."

Peter looked at the angel. He looked at the sleeping guards. He looked at the empty chains. A wonderful dream, indeed! he thought.

The angel slipped through the bars of the cell door and motioned for Peter to follow. Peter tried to slip through, but his full fisherman figure got in the way.

Chuckling, the angel reached up and snapped out two of the metal bars.

Peter sucked in his belly and tried again. Finally, with a shove and a grunt, he burst through.

He started down the hall and then remembered with a shock that two guards were always stationed outside his cell. Peter stopped and turned around slowly. He wondered for a moment if this dream would turn into a nightmare.

The guards were there, all right. Standing to attention. But their eyes stared blindly ahead. And in their hands, where their spears should have been, the angel was placing the iron bars he had snapped from the cell door.

The angel stood between them, his arms crossed and his head tossed back, laughing a laugh that Peter might have called naughty, had he not known it came from heaven.

"An amazing dream!" Peter said.

The angel slipped past him and headed down a long hall towards the prison gates, waving for Peter to follow. Together they crept, the tiny bright angel, toes barely touching the floor, and his dark-cloaked shadow, lumbering behind on flat fisherman feet.

As they approached the first gate, the angel whispered into Peter's ear, "Do you like to play make-believe?"

Make-believe? When Peter was a small boy—smaller even than this angel—he used to pretend he was with his father out on the sea. He'd drag a piece of old net across the beach and haul in catches of flat stone fish. "Sure," Peter whispered. He liked to play make-believe.

"Good," said the angel. "You can pretend to be Amos, the old man who cleans out the cells. It should get us past the next guards."

"But I don't look anything like him," Peter protested. And I don't sound anything like him. What will I do if they ask me a question?"

"Just stoop over," ordered the little angel, "and put your hand on your back, as if it's sore. Now walk very slowly, as if you're afraid of falling down."

The angel pulled Peter's cloak over his head, making a hood to hide his face. "That's good. That's very good," he sniggered. "And don't worry about how you'll sound. Leave the talking to me."

Peter stooped and shuffled his way to the first gate.

But when he saw the guards, he wondered if it wasn't time to pinch himself and wake up from this dream.

Too late! A voice was already echoing out from somewhere inside his cloak. "Evening, boys," it quivered. "Another late night and—oh!—my back is killing me. 'Old Amos,' my wife says, 'you're too old to be scrubbing out those cells. Think of your rheumatism. Think of your legs. Think of the diseases you could pick up in that place!'

" 'Ah, but old Agatha,' I says back, 'the king needs me. The prisoners need me. Those guards—those brave young boys—they need me. And they're always so kind to me,' I says, 'very kind indeed.' "

One of the guards swung open the gate, and the other chuckled and reached into his belt. "Here you go, old man," he said. And he tossed Peter a small coin.

Peter started to reach out and catch it, but the angel quietly slapped his hand and whispered, "No. Let it drop. Now stoop to pick it up, but watch out for the guard's . . ."

BOOT! The guard's foot found Peter's behind and sent him sprawling.

The angel made small clucking noises inside Peter's cloak. "Tsk! Tsk! You boys *will* have your fun."

Peter climbed slowly and shakily to his feet. Then, chased by the guards' laughter, he skittered down the hall like an old spider.

"Never mind them," grinned the angel. "We'll have the last laugh."

By the time they reached the main gate, the one that led out of the prison and into the city, Peter was really enjoying his dream. The gate was massive so there was no need for any guards. Who could possibly break out of it? And who would want to break in?

Peter looked down at the angel and smiled. "Now what?" he said. "Let me guess. You just wave your hand and the gate swings open, right?"

The angel smiled back. "You're catching on." And with a giggle, he waved his hand. The gate swung open.

Together they walked through dark, deserted streets towards the house where Peter's friends were praying. And they filled those silent streets with their laughter.

They sniggered as they imagined how those guards would feel when they woke up.

They cheered when they thought about the reaction of Peter's worried friends.

And they snorted and guffawed as they pictured the look on King Herod's face when he heard the news.

"This has been great fun," said the angel as they reached the house of Peter's friends. "But now it's time for me to go."

"And time for me to wake up, I suppose," Peter sighed.

"No," the angel giggled as a beam of light shot down from the stars. "That's the best joke of all. You've been awake the whole time!" And with a snap of his fingers, he slid up the beam and out of sight.

Peter stood there for a moment staring up into the

sky. A cool breeze ruffled his hair and sent a shiver down his spine. He looked around. The street was empty.

Then he reached out and touched the solid stone wall of his friends' house. He rapped his knuckles against their hard wooden door. And he listened to the astonished voice of the young girl who opened it.

"It's Peter!" she gasped. "It's Peter! He's free!" And she ran inside to tell the others, leaving Peter standing outside.

So it was true. And not a dream at all. The guards. The broken bars. The angel.

Peter shook his head. He had escaped. he could hardly believe it. What a night! What a rescue! What a joke!

Then a smile found its way onto his free fisherman's face. And he stepped inside to share the joke with his friends.

At the beginning of Acts, *chapter 12, it looks as if evil King Herod is in charge and nothing can stop him. He put to death James, one of Jesus' close friends and followers. Then he decided to go after bigger fish by hauling in Peter, the leader of this group that wouldn't stop talking about Jesus. Herod intended to have Peter killed as well. But he had to wait, for there was a religious festival in progress, and the execution could not take place until it was over.*

That gave God time to play the practical joke described in this story. A joke, because it left Peter's friends with silly, amazed smiles on their faces. practical, because it freed Peter to go on preaching about Jesus and showed King Herod who was really in charge. And, if you read between the lines of the Bible account in Acts, *I think you might just see a shadow of that mischievous angel grin.*

$\mathcal{T}$HE ANGEL
IN THE STORM

They stood on the deck together: the merchant, the captain, the soldier and the prisoner.

"I'm for going on," the merchant argued. "It's the only way to save the ship. If another storm brews up, this little port we're in won't begin to protect us."

"Aye," agreed the captain. "Winter's coming, and the stormy season with it. There are safer ports on the other side of the island."

"Just so long as we get there," the soldier added impatiently. "We should have been to Rome by now."

"Well, if you ask me," said the prisoner staring out at the dark skies, "if we set off in this weather, we're going to lose this ship—and most of us as well. We're safe here. I say we should just stay put." Then he turned and hobbled away.

The other three watched him go, watched his skinny

legs and hunched back and unruly hair disappear into the fog.

"Who does he think he is?" snapped the merchant. "This is my ship, and I say where she goes."

"Bandy-legged landlubber!" the captain huffed. "What does he know about the sea?"

"His name is Paul," the soldier said. "I'm taking him to Rome to stand trial before Caesar. Seems he's caused trouble in Jerusalem teaching about some new god called Jesus."

"Well," the merchant muttered, "he'll need all the help his new god can give him if he doesn't keep his nose out of other people's business. Captain, let's shove off."

And so the boat left the port and headed out to sea.

A week later, they were on deck again. But no one was standing this time.

They held onto the ropes. They held onto the rails. They held onto anything sturdy enough to keep them from being blown into the water.

"A Northeaster!" shouted the captain. "The fiercest storm there is. But in all my seafaring days, I've never seen one so fierce as this."

"We've done all we can," moaned the merchant. "But the storm is still driving us. We're miles off course, heading straight for the deadly swamps along Africa's shore. There's no hope for us."

"No hope?" asked the soldier.

"Oh, I wouldn't say that," answered the prisoner. In

many ways he looked just like the other three. His clothes were drenched, his hair lay slick against his head. And he, too, was bent double by the fierce winds and rain. But where the other three wore worried frowns, he sported a broad smile.

"Everything is going to be fine," shouted Paul against the storm. "I've just seen an angel. Over there. On the other side of the ship. His eyes were lightning. His voice thunder. His hair wild like the waves.

" 'Paul,' he told me, 'don't be afraid. You will be safe—you and everyone else on board. You're meant to appear before Caesar, and so you will. You have God's word on it.'

"So, you see," Paul smiled, "all we need to do is stay on the ship and trust God. He will take care of the rest." Then Paul staggered away.

"He's been out to sea too long," muttered the merchant.

"Barnacles for brains," the captain sputtered, "that's what he's got. Everybody saved? It'll take the luck of Neptune to see even ten of us safely on shore."

"I don't know," mused the soldier. "He was the one who told us not to leave in the first place."

Seven more days passed. Driven by the wind, the ship drifted blind through a moonless night. There were sailors on deck, scurrying about in the dark like rats.

"There's land ahead, captain," the first sailor squeaked. "We've checked and the water's getting shallow."

"But there's sure to be rocks ahead, too," squeaked another. "We wouldn't be able to steer past them. The wind's too fierce. The waves too high. We'll wreck for sure."

"Gather round, lads," the captain called. "I have a plan."

Several moments later, the sailors scurried to the side of the ship and started to load the lifeboat.

"Quiet now, lads," the captain whispered. "We don't want to wake anyone. Before long, we'll have this little boat through the rocks and be safe on shore."

And they might have done just that ... if someone hadn't been watching them.

He might have been out for a bit of fresh air. Maybe

he couldn't sleep. Or perhaps he hoped to meet another angel.

In any case, Paul saw them loading the boat and ran to tell the soldier. "You've got to stop them," he warned. "In order for the angel's promise to come true, we must all stay on the ship."

The soldier looked hard at Paul, then he called his men. Together they raced to the deck.

"Hold it right there," he called to the sailors. "Where do you think you're going?"

"Ah, well . . ." mumbled the captain. "We were just off to drop an anchor from the front of the ship. Keep her from drifting, you know. Right, lads?"

The sailors squeaked. Their heads bobbed up and down.

The soldier pointed at Paul. "This man tells me you were about to abandon ship."

"What? Him?" the captain grunted. "The man who sees angels? He's crazy as a loon."

The soldier glanced into the lifeboat and spotted the ship's remaining food and water. He lifted the bundle out.

"Perhaps he is crazy as a loon," said the solder, swinging his sword through one of the ropes from which the lifeboat hung. "Perhaps he's not," he continued, cutting through another. "What I do know is that all of us are riding out this storm together." And he cut through the last rope.

Together the men watched the empty lifeboat

bounce and bob away until it was swallowed by the dark sea. After that, no one could go back to sleep.

"Listen," Paul announced to them all. "I saw an angel. With a face like the moon. Hands big as clams. White gull wings. He promised we would all come safely to land. The shore is near, so we need to build up our strength. Now is the time to dig into our remaining supplies, to eat and get ready for landing."

The merchant looked at the soldier. "He's a strange one, all right. He's got some nerve."

The soldier looked at the merchant. "Yes, he has. But he hasn't steered us wrong so far."

The captain did not dare to say a thing.

"All right," called the merchant. "Eat whatever you want. Then throw what's left overboard and get some sleep."

So Paul gave thanks to God, and together they ate.

Next morning they all stood on the deck. But the deck was falling apart. The ship had struck a sandbar.

"We've run aground!" called the captain.

"We'll have to swim for it!" cried the merchant.

The soldier called for his men. "Gather the prisoners," he ordered. 'We need to swim for shore."

"But sir," asked one of his men, "what if they escape?"

"Yes," said another. "The punishment is death for the soldier who lets a prisoner escape. Unless, of course, the prisoner dies."

"That's right," agreed a third. "If they die, they can't escape. Why don't we just kill the prisoners right now?"

The soldier looked at the prisoners. They were a raggle-taggle bunch. Except for the strange one—the man who'd seen an angel.

Gull wings. Lightning eyes. Hair like the waves.

Had Paul really seen such a messenger from heaven, the solder wondered. Well, his words had come true, hadn't they? He'd been right about the storm, about the sailors—about most everything, really.

"No," the soldier ordered. "We've come this far together. We'll finish the journey together, too. Ready? One. Two. Three. JUMP!"

They stood on the beach together. Every single one of them. All present and accounted for.

"Well, we made it," sighed the merchant. "I just wish I could say the same for my ship."

"We're alive!" shouted the captain as he kissed the ground. "Who could have guessed it? Who could have guessed it?"

A green wave curled up against the shore. A gull cried overhead. And in the distance, lightning flashed.

The soldier watched the wave and the gull and the lightning. Then he looked across the beach to where Paul was praying.

"The prisoner could have," he said softly, "that's who. The strange one. The man who saw the angel."

By the time of the shipwreck, which is described in chapter 27 of Acts, Paul had already made three long journeys to tell the ancient world about Jesus. And many of those journeys were on the water. So Paul knew how dangerous the sea could be, especially during the stormy winter season. And he was probably just as surprised as the others when the angel told him they would all survive the storm.

But survive it they did. And afterwards, they made their way to Rome for Paul's trial. While Paul waited for the trial, he had visitors, and he shared the story about Jesus with them and with his guards. He also wrote letters to churches he had started on those earlier trips.

After that, we lose track of Paul. There are plenty of stories and guesses about what happened to him. But for all practical purposes, the rest of his life is a mystery—like meeting an angel at sea.